Luis y Sofía

Spanish Stories for Primary School Pupils, Level 1

7 Specially Written Short Stories for Beginning Learners

Barbara Scanes and Jenny Bell

> For instructions on how to download your free audio files and printable resources for the stories, please see page 57.

Contents
1. Buenos diás 1
2. Me llamo Sofía 9
3. ¿Cuántas galletas? 17
4. Tengo seis años 25
5. Tengo un hermano 33
6. Muchos caramelos 41
7. Un caramelo rojo 49

Downloadable files
The downloadable files include an audio recording of the story and vocabulary list for each story (eg. LSS1-1-STORY-AUDIO.mp3 and LSS1-1-VOCAB-AUDIO.mp3) as well as a pdf file containing the English translations for all 7 stories (LSS1-TRANSLATIONS-PDF.pdf)

Published by Brilliant Publications Limited, Unit 10, Sparrow Hall Farm, Edlesborough, Dunstable, LU6 2ES.
www.brilliantpublications.co.uk
The name 'Brilliant Publications' is a registered trade mark.

Written by Barbara Scanes and Jenny Bell
Illustrated by Paul Hutchinson
© Barbara Scanes, Jenny Bell and Brilliant Publications Limited 2018
ISBN printed book: 978-1-78317-374-7
ISBN PDF book: 978-1-78317-378-5

First printed and published in the UK as 7 individual books in 2018. First printed and published in this collection in 2024.

The right of Barbara Scanes and Jenny Bell to be identified as the authors of this work has been asserted by themselves in accordance with the Copyright, Designs and Patents Act 1988.

All rights reserved. Apart from any use permitted under UK copyright law, no part of this publication may be reproduced or transmitted in any form or by any means, electronic or mechanical, including photocopying and recording, or held within any information storage and retrieval system, without permission in writing from the publishers or under licence from the Copyright Licensing Agency Limited. Further details of such licenses (for reprographic reproduction) may be obtained from the Copyright Licensing Agency Limited, 5th Floor, Shackleton House, 4 Battle Bridge Lane, London SE1 2HX (https://cla.co.uk).

Buenos días

Vocabulario

buenos días	good morning/hello
escuchad	listen
levantaos	get up
mirad	look
un cocodrilo	a crocodile
no	no
soy yo	it's me
mamá	mum
ahora	now
por favor	please

Me llamo Sofía

Vocabulario

hola	hello
¿qué tal?	how are you?/are you OK?/how are things?
estoy bien	I'm fine/things are fine
bien	well/fine
gracias	thank you
¿cómo te llamas?	what's your name?
me llamo...	my name is...
¿y tú?	and you?
¿estás bien?	are you OK?
qué mal	things are bad
viene mi mamá	mum's coming
adiós	goodbye

¿Cuántas galletas?

Vocabulario

¿cuántas galletas?	how many biscuits?
tengo	I have
tienes	you have
una galleta	a biscuit
unas galletas	some biscuits
sí	yes
son	they are
para	for
mis muñecas	my dolls
pero	but
sólo	only
entonces	then
muchas/muchos	lots of
una/uno	one
dos	two
tres	three
cuatro	four
cinco	five
seis	six
siete	seven
ocho	eight
nueve	nine
diez	ten
y	and
¿cuántos?/¿cuántas?	how many?
mí	me

Tengo seis años

Vocabulario

¿cuántos años tienes?	how old are you?
tengo seis años	I'm six (years old)
tienes siete años	you're seven (years old)
¿tienes siete años?	are you seven (years old)?
dentro de poco	soon
es	it is
mi cumpleaños	my birthday
de momento	at the moment
(tú) eres	you are
un bebé	a baby

Tengo un hermano

Vocabulario

¿tienes?	have you (got)?
hermanos	brothers/brothers and sisters
una hermana	a sister
una hermana pequeña	a little sister
un hermano	a brother
dos hermanos	two brothers
(ella) tiene tres años	she is three (years old)
tener	to have
me gustaría	I would like
¿quién es?	who is that?/who is it?
mi hermano	my brother
(él) es	he is
tonto	silly (masculine)
ser	to be
hija única	only child (feminine)

Muchos caramelos

Vocabulario

Sofía tiene	Sofía has
un caramelo	a sweet
unos caramelos	some sweets
y a mí	me too
¿cuántos ... tienes?	how many ... do you have?
once	eleven
doce	twelve
trece	thirteen
catorce	fourteen
quince	fifteen
dieciséis	sixteen
diecisiete	seventeen
dieciocho	eighteen
diecinueve	nineteen
veinte	twenty
cero	zero
para ti	for you

Un caramelo rojo

Vocabulario

rojo	red
azul	blue
verde	green
amarillo	yellow
naranja	orange
rosa	pink
morado	purple
marrón	brown
cerrad los ojos	close your eyes
abrid los ojos	open your eyes
ganar	to win
adivinad	guess
el color	the colour
qué color falta	which colour is missing
es el rojo	it's the red (one)
esto es un rollo	it's rubbish/that's rubbish

Download instructions

To download your free resources for **Luis y Sofía Spanish Stories for Primary School Pupils, Level 1**:

Go to: **https://www.brilliantpublications.education**

You will need to set up a log in with an email address and password if you do not already have one for the https://www.brilliantpublications.education website. (Please note: you will need to set up a new account on this website to download your files, even if you already have an account on our main website.)

Your username may contain: letters, numbers and the special characters * - _ . @

You will be asked to confirm your email address by clicking the validation link emailed to you when you register.

Don't forget to check in spam/junk if you do not see an email from us.

We have introduced 2-factor authorisation on this website to make it more secure. This means that whenever you log in, you will be sent a numerical authorisation code by email which you must copy and paste into the welcome page on the website. The authentication code only lasts 1 hour.

Once logged on, choose the **Spanish** category and click on the cover for **Luis y Sofía Spanish Stories for Primary School Pupils, Level 1**.

Your unique password for the downloads is: **LS56gWpm9**

The downloaded filename will be **Spanish-Stories-Level-1.zip**

Please note, the password will be changed at regular intervals so make sure you save a copy of the files once you have downloaded them.

If you experience any difficulties with downloading your files, please email info@brilliantpublications.co.uk and we will get back to you as soon as possible.

Depending on the speed of your internet and the size of the download, it may take some time for the download to complete. To avoid problems, please make sure that your computer does not go to sleep during the download.

Note: We test the software on PCs and Apple Macs, but there are too many different types of hardware in schools for us to be able to test it on every device owned by schools.

www.ingramcontent.com/pod-product-compliance
Lightning Source LLC
Chambersburg PA
CBHW040054100426
42734CB00043B/3279